From Burned Out

TO
FIRED
UP

PRAISE FOR
FROM BURNED OUT TO FIRED UP

"Liz Rosado-McGrath is a true expert on the ins and outs of being a teacher; the trials and hardships, celebrations and joy. In this book she gives teachers tools to transform being a teacher into positive power and fulfillment with her joyful knowledge and wisdom."

Kim Somers-Egelsee
Bestselling Author of *Getting Your Life to a 10 Plus*

"Because of Liz Rosado-McGrath I have learned to grow my students more than I ever thought I could. I recently have been looking at my data and looking at my students' growth. Due to the techniques and tips you taught me, many of my students have grown a whole year in one semester."

Natalie Duzich

"Liz Rosado-McGrath's mentoring has definitely influenced my teaching this year! Thanks for your help."

Andrew Rodriguez

"Liz Rosado-McGrath has the ability to bring people together for a common purpose and excel at getting the best out of them. You trust them to work hard and they do not disappoint because you have empowered them without controlling their every move. You are also passionate about what you do and are constantly seeking to learn more."

Agelia Durand

"Working with Ms. McGrath has been a Godsend. She taught me how to truly see where to meet my students. I have grown as a literacy leader within my campus."

Bertha Munoz

"It's inspiring to witness the passion Liz Rosado-McGrath has for empowering teachers to make a difference in their students' capacity to learn. As a book coach and publisher, I know that one cannot afford to let stress cause burnout, or diminish the quality of your work."

Susie Augustin
Bestselling Author of *Writing to Wow!*

From Burned Out

TO FIRED UP

Teachers Reignite Their Passion to Inspire!

Elizabeth Rosado-McGrath, MEd

!
GET
BRANDED
PRESS

Get Branded Press
Newport Beach, CA 92663
www.GetBrandedPress.com

Limits of Liability and Disclaimer of Warranty.
The author and publisher shall not be liable for your misuse of this material. This book is strictly for informational and educational purposes.

Warning – Disclaimer.
The purpose of this book is to educate and entertain. The author and/or publisher do not guarantee that anyone following these techniques, suggestions, tips, ideas, or strategies will become successful. The author and/or publisher shall have neither liability nor responsibility to anyone with respect to anyone with respect to any loss or damage caused, or alleged to be caused, directly or indirectly by the information contained in this book.

ISBN 978-1-944807-01-6 paperback
Library of Congress Cataloging-in-Publishing Data is available upon request.
Printed in the United States of America
First Printing, 2016

Editing by Taylor Augustin www.GetBrandedPress.com
Cover & Interior Design by Kate Korniienko-Heidtman
Back Cover Photography by Studio One to One

This book is dedicated to my third grade teacher,
Mrs. Roberta Jones.
You gave me what every great teacher
gives to their students...
HOPE.

ACKNOWLEDGMENTS

I would like to send out my deep gratitude for all teachers everywhere who bravely create miracles in their classrooms on a moment-by-moment basis. You are the inspiration behind the content in this book. My intention is to create more of us who find and regularly feel the joy within ourselves so that we may more deeply connect with our students.

Thank you to so many of you who provided feedback when I shared my questions regarding what was burning you out and what made you feel empowered. Your responses were painfully honest and raw. I truly appreciate you taking the time to respond and with such vulnerability.

To my colleagues from whom I have learned so much over the years, I have not only become a better educator, but a better person. Sara Hannes, Nolia Rohde, Martha Martinez, Gretchen Holtsinger, Agelia Durand, Karen Sanders, Virginia Aguilar, Hortencia Vega, Judy Wallis and many others. Each of you have taught me so many vital lessons. I am forever grateful for our paths crossing and the wisdom you have brought to my life.

This book would not have seen the light of day if not for Kim Somers-Egelsee and my editor and publisher, Susie Augustin and Get Branded Press. Kim, your coaching and always positive encouragement are something everyone on the planet should have in their life. Susie, without your patience and persistence this would all still be just a big idea. You both are amazing!

Finally, to my family, thank you for being here for me. My dad whose final coherent words were, "Good luck with your writing", my mom who always saw the bigger picture of my life, Kristina and Alex who are always in my corner, and Paul, the personal editor and humble defender of all that is good, I love you.

TABLE OF CONTENTS

FOREWORD

A powerful and poignant examination and response to the ongoing issues within our educational system and those who spend their lives in service to the future of our world, the children. I have always been passionate about creating a world where our children can thrive in powerful and positive ways. Liz Rosado-McGrath addresses the concerns and everyday realities of the experiences within the organizations our children grow up in. One of my favorite lines in her book, "When you pull back the curtain," describes what you see behind closed doors. The ongoing isolation of many educators is a large concern. Facilitating active approaches and practices which support a healthy teaching and learning environment for all involved, are essential in today's shifting educational paradigms.

This book is timely and pertinent. I strongly recommend this for all teachers, school administrators, and parents.

Warmly,
Shajen Joy Aziz, M.Ed., M.A.

Shajen Joy Aziz, M.Ed. is an award winning international best-selling author, with a dual master's degree in education and psychology. Twenty years as a progressive educator, school administrator, teacher and counselor, paved the way for her to become a leader within the transformational and peace-building communities. Shajen is a filmmaker, motivational trainer and speaker. She is a mother, teacher, author and co-creator of the international bestselling book and film *Discover the Gift – It's Why We're Here.* www.DiscovertheGift.com

INTRODUCTION

A segment on the evening news first inspired me to become a teacher. The story was about the critical shortage of teachers in the area of bilingual and ESL education. It stopped me dead in my tracks. I knew having worked with children in a boarder town previously that this is where I needed and truly wanted to be. In order to make this happen, I enrolled in a post-bac program to work towards my teaching credentials, as I had already graduated college. From there I moved to San Antonio and participated in an alternate certification program where I received my certification. I felt relieved and very excited when I finally received my certification. Anyone will tell you how extremely difficult their first year of teaching is, but when you are concurrently taking graduate classes as a part of the process, it is rather grueling.

My first teaching job was as a kindergarten teacher in a southern school district in San Antonio, TX. Parts of the job were to be expected, while others were not. It was far more challenging when it came to the outside of the classroom requirements, i.e., creating lesson plans, meetings, professional development, etc. The teaching experience has vastly changed since I first started. There are so many additional requirements when it comes to accountability. Teachers are expected to perform like master teachers very early on in their careers.

My most memorable experience with a student was when I was working with a struggling reader as part of a specialized reading program. We were videotaping her reading aloud before the sessions began, but she was so quiet you could barely hear her speak. She had her hands below the table and she wouldn't even hold the book. When the reading intervention was complete because she made grade level progress, we videotaped her again. I knew she was doing great but the first time I watched the clips side by side, tears came streaming down my face. She was animated this time, changing voices with the characters; she held the book up and sat up straight in her chair. It wasn't just that she could read now, her entire perception of herself had changed in a matter of weeks. I was and still am in awe. Having experiences like this is what inspires me as a teacher. Even more so, I love being able to support fellow teachers. Working side by side with classroom teachers and helping them become confident, joyful, expert educators!

According to the 2010 census, there were 7.3 million teachers in the US. In fact, the National Center for Educational Statistics informs us that about 3.3 million of those are currently teaching full time. And while finding the number of teachers currently teaching in the world remains a bit elusive, what we do know from a recent UNESCO report is that 6.8 million teachers would need to be recruited by 2015 in order to provide the right education to all primary school-age children worldwide. This number is more poignant when we consider approximately 40-50 percent of all teachers leave the profession within their first five years. Even more alarming, in the past two decades, the rate of attrition among first year teachers has increased by about 33 percent.

It is for all of these reasons and more that I believe the premise for this book is not just important, but critical. The field of education is currently at a crossroads and there are many factors contributing to the number of teachers who not only leave the profession, but worse, stay in it and are UNHAPPY. Single assessment accountability ratings, teacher firings, evaluations, budget cuts, and dysfunctional disagreement over best practices are leaving many educators in a state of despair. How educators cope with all of these changes and how they choose to be impacted by them is what I am exploring and ultimately aiming to help transform.

If I could instigate change, I would like to see each and every new teacher in the profession receive a true mentor teacher over a two-year period. This would be someone who could support them professionally and emotionally while they find their sea legs. I contribute to this change we so desperately need by providing teachers with educational tools while at the same time, modeling how to manage emotions.

I get burnt out from temporarily allowing the sometimes crush of everyday life to bore a hole in me until I take a deep breath and recall how to release it all. There are so many things that fire me up! Being a part of creating and sustaining a community of educators who celebrate successes, encourage each other through vulnerabilities, and who model emotional management for our students is an amazing thing to be part of. Imagine a generation of youth who grow up consciously knowing how to turn down the volume on anger and frustration! It is my wish that through this book, you to will learn how to turn your burnt out sessions into something amazing. Get fired up!

If this resonates with you and you truly desire to reignite your passion to inspire...I extend an invitation to you to continue along this journey.

Because we know all learning is social, I would encourage you to find and/or create a group of colleagues (large or small), and use this book in a book study format. With scheduled meetings, it is significantly easier to continue our own growth while we support others. Regular meetings also create opportunities to solidify new habits into becoming an integral part of who we are. Try it out and share your results. I am eager to hear from you and get your feedback.

FROM BURNED OUT

"A good teacher is like a candle –
it consumes itself to light the way for others."
~ Author Unknown

Have you ever felt like you were sitting in the center of a human-sized vise? There you are, smack dab in the middle while some external force continues to turn the handle...exerting more and more pressure. Suddenly you feel like you are about to explode and indeed, you are exploding. And yet, like a freshly squeezed orange, what comes out is what's inside – all the good stuff. It might not feel good at the time, but what needs to emerge is all the good to great that is YOU!

It is no secret that teachers everywhere are feeling stressed and to varying degrees, burned out. It doesn't matter if you are new to the profession or if you have many years of experience under your belt. Data and research inform us of this, in addition to the many of you who were kind enough to respond to my inquiries below.

- What are the top 5-7 issues in education today?
- Would you name a few disempowered feelings related to teaching?
- What do you feel would make things better for you/other teachers moving forward?

I was truly amazed at the outpouring of responses and the brutally frank manner in which these teachers shared their experiences.

Before I pull back the curtain on the responses and engage in deepening our understanding of the issues, I would first like to clarify a few things. First, I am a teacher. I am a classroom teacher who gradually moved into several administrative roles, and currently serve in a in consulting capacity. Effective and targeted professional development (including teacher induction programs) is critical to teacher quality and longevity. However, I also believe we can no longer afford to omit attending to the affective needs of teachers AT THE SAME TIME.

In fact, teachers who are unhappy with their jobs miss significantly more days of work than their happier colleagues. A recent Gallup poll found that teachers who feel less engaged with their work were more likely to report that poor health kept them from their normal teaching routine. Poor health and increased absenteeism take a definite toll not just on teachers, but students.

While we all face varying degrees of personal stress from time to time, *the ability to manage it* is critical for teachers. I recently had the distinct privilege of meeting a dedicated high school science teacher in the Houston area. She attended one of my sessions that included a classroom follow-up built into the contract. After observing her highly skilled lessons in action, we had a chance to debrief. During our professional conversation, she shared with me that not too long ago her mother had passed away. By any standard, losing one's mother is a difficult and stressful event to live through. But in her case, it didn't stop there. Shortly thereafter, her husband took his own life, followed by her father having a machinery accident on his ranch. As she was getting ready to leave town to visit her father in the hospital, she received a call from child protective services. Her niece had left her 3-year-old daughter alone in her apartment for three days, and the case worker needed to know if they should place the child into foster care, or if she wanted to have temporary custody. This is absolutely a case of extreme stress. However, my point is that when teachers are experiencing such things, it is critical to provide support so that they feel better as soon as possible, lest their interactions with students suffer.

This section of the book is the shortest by intention. Why? Because it is energetically heavy and not the point of improving our practice. Having said that, we cannot move forward and transform into something bigger and better without acknowledging where we are at the current time. So take your seats and let's establish a baseline for the current state of affairs in teaching – but stay tuned for the best tasting orange juice you've ever had!

IN THE BEGINNING...

Many of us begin our teaching careers with stars in our eyes, fire in our bellies, and passion in our hearts. We enter the profession brimming with optimism, waiting to receive our first group of students and charge full steam ahead. Somehow, we feel we bring necessary hope to the schools of today, and may revel a bit in the important role a teacher plays in the lives of others. And yet, over time, those feelings of joy and positivity can become a bit diminished, or may disappear altogether. The "realities" of teaching are not long to emerge, causing us to question why we selected this career, or in some cases, leave the profession entirely.

My intention here is to explain how this dramatic shift can occur, and detail some of these *realities*. While I certainly have my own opinions, I found the best way to explore this was to talk with experienced teachers. Many of the educators who shared information with me did so boldly, eloquently, and fearlessly. So to begin this section, I would like to share the most common responses in the order they occurred.

Here are some of the issues related to *WHY* teachers indicate they have become burned out: *Testing, Time, Incoherent Curriculum, Lack of Good Professional Development, Mismatch Between Background of Teachers and Students, and Ineffective Leadership.*

Let's begin with the most frequent reason given for burnout.

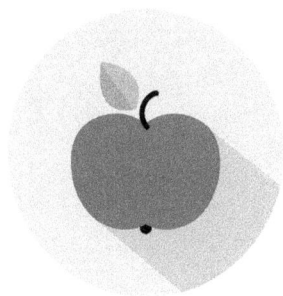

TESTING

As I feel the crushing stress of standardized testing in schools today, I'm still blown away by the number of responses I received, coupled with commentary. Here are some examples:

"There is a great amount of pressure on teachers and students over standardized test results."

"There is pressure everywhere for your kids to pass the exams and if they don't, you are fired or put on a growth plan – it is also making the kids sick. I have known many kids that get sick (throw up/can't sleep) just thinking about taking the test."

"Over testing – period."

"Too much relentless testing."

I remember serving as the testing coordinator at a campus where I was working in an administrative capacity. During the training we received, we were actually given instructions on what to do with test forms in the event students vomited on them. For a moment it's comical to think of and then one realizes the culture of testing has indeed become extreme. While none of the teachers I communicated with expressed a desire to do away with testing entirely, they indicated the focus and level of high importance given to the results were very much out of balance. Testing results, as suggested by many, should be measured by growth and not by an arbitrary yardstick. Finally, when the interpretation of testing results falls into the high stakes category, the work environment is indeed out of balance. Out of balance is a clear predictor of stress.

TIME

While time is and has always been something of a nemesis for teachers, I do believe it has become more of a villain born from its parent – *TESTING.* Time, or lack thereof, is attributed to many different issues. For example: adequate time to teach given the testing schedule, time to effectively and thoroughly plan, time for re-teaching, time lost to too many unproductive meetings, conference time, etc.

Several respondents mentioned that because a current major focus in education is individual differentiation, there really needs to be additional planning time to better account for all students. A fair parallel may be to think of time as being like energy. It can't be created or destroyed, it can only be redirected. And therein lies the stress. If one cannot see a way to redirect or manage their time, they will tend to remain in the pressure cooker at the mercy of internal temperature buildup.

Here are some of the comments I received regarding the issue of time. Did I mention time? Because of the need to differentiate instruction, the time teachers need to plan well is multiplied.

"Too much testing equals not enough time to teach."

"Planning TIME? What is that? Meetings every day during planning time, STAT meetings, ARDs, team meetings, etc. etc. etc."

"I really do feel like with the number of new objectives at _____ grade, we are rushing through too fast, and not giving students adequate time to practice and develop that deeper knowledge that we are striving for."

INCOHERENT CURRICULUM

One definition of the word *incoherent* is "unable to express one's self clearly." This is a fine illustration of trying to work with a curriculum that doesn't allow teachers to align information in an articulate manner, so that students can more easily synthesize new learning. How does this happen? According to feedback, teachers are frustrated with shifting standards and their local jurisdiction's interpretation of them. Some administrators focus more on certain aspects, while others do not. Teachers are expected to stop using certain materials in favor of new ones that support the updated standards, etc.

I am also including in this section the topic of *TECHNOLOGY*. As this relates directly to the issue of curriculum, in so many places teachers have referred to it as incoherent. For many the challenges are as follows:

- How to integrate technology into the content area.
- Hardware problems – many are using antiquated computers and software that no longer function.
- Lack of access to computers or still trying to schedule time in a lab.
- Technology doesn't work, gets broken, or isn't supported by other technology in the district.

Lastly, there may be gaps or misinterpretations of the curriculum as it relates to state testing. This clearly creates a disconnect between teaching and assessment.

LACK OF QUALITY PROFESSIONAL DEVELOPMENT

The topic of *Professional Development* was mentioned repeatedly in the responses I received from teachers. While frequent, there were variations in the reasons why it was problematic. For some, there was never enough professional development. In many places school districts have severely curtailed the number of days allocated for this in their yearly calendar. Dedicated PD days that in the past took place before a new school year began, have now become almost eliminated, mostly due to budget cuts. Whereas teachers could previously obtain new information on curriculum updates, materials, testing information, etc., *before* receiving their new students, this now must be scheduled after the school year begins, placing everyone behind the eight ball. Refer to the previous section related to Time Management.

A different facet of problematic professional development is one of either inferior quality, or a misalignment with current objectives. Given the time constraints teachers have already identified, there are few things as wasteful as being required to attend sessions that offer no return in value. Respondents said at times the sessions were not related to identified needs at the campus, and other times it was an issue of poor quality. Interestingly, several participants mentioned a desire for professional development opportunities that would focus on improved communication between both administrators and teachers as well as schools and their communities.

MISMATCH BETWEEN BACKGROUND OF TEACHERS AND STUDENTS

Nationwide, public schools are becoming more economically and racially diverse. In fact, in 21 states and the District of Columbia, more than 50 percent of students now qualify for free and reduced lunch. This, coupled with the reality that the demographics of the teacher workforce have not kept pace with these changes, have contributed to some teachers admittedly feeling ill-prepared to address these issues.

While certainly not all teachers struggle with students who come from backgrounds different from their own, many have honestly shared that they would appreciate more training and information on how best to approach instruction for these students. This is especially true for teachers new to the profession. Several teachers shared that many of their low income students experience daily difficulties related to hunger, health, and violence.

INEFFECTIVE LEADERSHIP

Sadly, lack of leadership is something that should not be an issue in any workplace, much less somewhere as important as our schools. This is especially true given the high needs and demands of so many students in US public schools today. One respondent said it best when she said there should be leadership based on vision that comes from resources and research, rather than personal beliefs.

Other respondents indicated a number of factors caused by the ineffectiveness of leaders: a lack of trust, disempowerment, and an overall joylessness in the workplace. This frequently leads to additional micromanaging, overall CYA syndrome, and breeds a dangerous repetitive cycle.

CONCLUSIONS

The previous listed topics contributing to teacher burnout were specifically mentioned because of their frequency within the responses and from patterns throughout the comments. There were other issues cited by teachers that contribute to feeling burned out, although shared less frequently. While not part of overall patterns, many of these are no less important. Here are some examples:

- Too much pressure for both students and teachers to "perform"
- Overcrowding in schools
- Decrepit facilities
- The increasing responsibility on teachers to be parents, nurses, counselors, etc.
- Isolation from peers
- Increasing needs of parents, limiting their ability to parent
- Parent incarceration
- Large caseloads for special education teachers and counselors
- General mindset in society today of entitlement (parent and student)
- Too many unproductive meetings
- Too many requests for teachers to serve on committees outside of teaching

I am certain that with additional input from the larger community of educators, we could add to this list. However, I am confident you are already feeling the heavy energy of all of this, and understand how these topics indeed contribute to feelings of burnout. When asked to name some disempowered feelings related to teaching, here are some of the responses I received (in no particular order):

- Loss of control
- Exhaustion
- Frustration
- Stress
- Burnout
- Joylessness
- Lack of trust
- Depression
- Failure
- Inability to take risks
- Disrespected
- Overwhelmed

Enough? Can you feel it now? Don't despair. When teachers were asked a follow-up question relating to what would make things better overall for them and other educators, they had plenty of great suggestions. I will include these toward the end of the book, as they will connect with the third section, Teachers Reignite Their Passion to Inspire.

However, in order to move forward, we need to get our arms around the current situation such as it is. It is important to fully acknowledge the impact of specific stressors in order to bring them to the surface and address them – this way they can be "seen", felt, and observed.

After reading through all of these school-related topics, please take a few moments to reflect on your own stress triggers and list them below. You will have opportunities throughout this book where you will engage in an interactive journaling format. Please do yourself a favor and do not skip these sections – here is where you are likely to encounter your growth mindset.

Is there something not mentioned previously that is a trigger of stress for you?

As with school-related triggers, what might be some personal contributors to stress that are currently presenting themselves in your life?

Please be sure to write down your responses to the above mentioned questions, as we will be addressing them in the next section, which explores how to manage and alleviate the energy drain they have on us.

SECTION 2

TO
FIRED
UP!

"You are after all, what you think.
Your emotions are the slaves to your thoughts,
and you are the slave to your emotions."
~ Elizabeth Gilbert

"COME GET THIS STUDENT FROM MY CLASSROOM PLEASE! HE JUST THREW A CHAIR AND ALMOST HIT ANOTHER STUDENT."

In my role as an assistant principal, there was no such thing as a typical day. While as an administrative team we would receive pleas like this occasionally, it wasn't very common to hear it coming from a first grade classroom. I collected my thoughts and walked briskly down the hallways. There was (let's call him) Elias, already in a fit of uncontrolled crying in the corner. The other students were huddled safely with the teacher on the other side of the room. I do not remember the exact words I used to coax him to walk with me back the office, but I recall precisely the presence of mind I summoned to communicate trust coupled with safety.

After arriving in my office, I calmly closed the door as his rants continued to escalate. He threw himself down on the floor, rolled around kicking and screaming while I sat in my chair, keeping one eye on him with the other on my computer screen. I remember being very thankful that my office door had a window so that when people walked by, they could see exactly what was going on, instead of something that likely sounded like a child being beaten. For about 15 extremely long minutes, Elias continued his tirade. Interestingly though, every time he would roll around and kick the furniture, he would turn and look up at me to see if I was watching. I made no attempt to interrupt this temper tantrum. I only ensured he would not hurt himself in the process.

When he realized I was not reacting in any way to his explosive behavior, he stood up, and in one sweeping motion with his arms, trashed every stack of paper and folders from my conference table onto the floor...while he watched my face. I continued to view him from one eye and keep the other on my computer screen. Finally, he plopped down in a heap on the floor and stopped crying. His breathing slowly began to return to normal and I said nothing for about 10 minutes. Once he had calmed down completely, we talked about what had prompted him to throw the chair, how it made him feel and more. We discussed consequences of behaviors and what should happen next. Finally, I very calmly asked him to please pick up the papers and folders from the floor and place them back on my conference table. Without one word of objection, he complied and said he was sorry.

I share this story not to say this approach is effective with every attempt, but to demonstrate that with an intentional response that is non-reactive, we are able to shift the flow of emotions both in ourselves and in others.

- Would you prefer to generate statements that do not originate in anger, so that an apology or something worse is necessary?
- Would you like to avoid getting into battles with students/parents/colleagues/personal friends and family and reduce your level of exhaustion?
- Is it possible to transform from being burned out into fired up?

I not only believe it is possible, I know it is probable by simply increasing our awareness in a few select areas:

- Understanding the role of thoughts and emotions
- Mirrors and their impact
- Intentional word choice
- Making decisions

THE ROLE OF THOUGHTS AND EMOTIONS IN OUR LIVES

This discussion actually becomes clearer when we begin with what is at the root of all thoughts and emotions: feelings. Our working definition of feelings is that they are sensations we perceive. We can perceive these through actual touch, or at times they are a physical awareness connected internally (mentally), meaning not via the five senses. Feelings come from our soul and originate from core sensations in the body. Once a feeling emerges, the message of this sensation is sent directly to our brain wherein we generate a thought about said feeling, and this thought then triggers an emotional response. So, in linear form it looks like this:

FEELING OR SENSATION →
BRAIN RECEIVES AND GENERATES A THOUGHT ABOUT
THE FEELING →
EMOTIONAL RESPONSE IS ASSIGNED MEANING/TRIGGER

When this process occurs in real time, it is happening in a matter of split seconds making it a challenge to interrupt and shift the result. *And when we are unaware of the process, we remain in a state of reactivity.* We react instead of respond to the very things that contribute to being and feeling burned out. So let's return to the example of Elias I shared earlier and briefly examine what a reactive response might have been.

I receive the urgent request to remove a student (first time to interact with this student – no previous history) from a classroom because he has chosen a physical response to his own emotional trigger – whatever that may have been. Once I receive this message, I might get a feeling in the pit of my stomach. As I walk briskly to the classroom, this sensation in my stomach may increase in intensity, so once I arrive the thought in my head could be, "This kid is so in for it...I can't believe he would hold an entire class hostage with his outburst!" The ensuing emotional response then is the meaning I assign to this thought – possibly anger. What would the likely outcome of the event have been if I was in an emotional state of anger (probably his emotional state as well) when I arrived to remove him? One could argue that it would have been a bit more explosive and potentially damaging for all of the students and the teacher.

So how can we break it down and choose our responses instead of allowing them to control us? Let's examine the equation in a bit more depth.

FEELING →
BRAIN RECEIVES AND GENERATES A THOUGHT ABOUT
THE FEELING →
EMOTIONAL RESPONSE IS ASSIGNED MEANING/
TRIGGERED BY US

The feelings and sensations we perceive are generated from something physical or from something inside ourselves. These are not things we can manage or control, however, they present themselves in order for us to process and ultimately to release them. It's what happens after this that we can directly impact, in order to feel better! Once the brain receives the message regarding the feeling, a thought is formed in response. So in reality, all events, feelings, or sensations are neutral – it's the thoughts we generate about our feelings that create how we feel and how we respond.

Here are some examples related to our previous scenario.

FEELING: Ache in the pit of my stomach as a result of the call to the classroom.

1. Possible thought generated by the brain – *"I can't believe this kid did this!"*
   → Emotional meaning assigned – *Anger*

2. Possible thought generated by the brain – *"I have 800 things I would rather be doing than this."*
   → Emotional meaning assigned – *Overwhelm*

3. Possible thought generated by the brain – *"If this kid is already doing things like this, I wonder what kind of a future he will have."*
   → Emotional meaning assigned – *Pessimism*

4. Possible thought generated by the brain – *"I wonder how I can best help this student and the situation in the classroom?"*
   → Emotional meaning assigned – *Hopeful*

5. Possible thought generated by the brain – *"I know I have the skill set to best facilitate this difficult situation in the classroom."*
   → Emotional meaning assigned – *Positive expectation/belief*

These are just five examples of different ways to think about and choose an emotional response to an initial feeling. Notice that each example contains an emotion that FEELS better (lighter) than the previous one. Therein lies the essence of what we are intending...how can we shift our thoughts and their impact on our emotions in order to transform the feeling of burnout to that of being fired up? The great news is that it is completely within our control to do so...we simply choose it and continue to practice and refine the process.

Emotional responses range along a continuum of low/heavy to moderate to pure joy. They tend to be clustered together in a scale like this:

- Joy, Freedom, Love, Passion
- Enthusiasm, Positive Expectation, Belief
- Hopefulness, Contentment
- Boredom, Pessimism, Frustration, Irritation
- Overwhelmed, Disappointment, Doubt, Worry
- Discouragement, Anger, Revenge
- Jealousy, Guilt, Insecurity
- Fear, Depression, Powerlessness

In order to improve our response to events, examine the process through this lens of

FEELING → THOUGHT → EMOTION

Think of a recent event from work where it evoked a feeling in you. It may be one of the items we mentioned in the previous section that contributes to burnout: testing, lack of adequate time, incoherent curriculum, etc., or you may have a different one of your own (from your list). Once you have an example in mind, let's walk through this process.

Choose from the list of emotional responses above to assign emotional meanings in the following activity.

Feeling: _____

1. Possible thought generated by the brain:

"_____

_____"

a. Emotional meaning assigned

_____

_____

2. Possible thought generated by the brain:

"_____

_____"

(Better-feeling thought)
a. Emotional meaning assigned

"_____

_____"

(Better-feeling emotion)

3. Possible thought generated by the brain:

"_____

_____"

(Better-feeling thought)
a. Emotional meaning assigned

"_____

_____"

(Better-feeling emotion)

Repeat this process two times using other scenarios from your list to reach for a better feeling, culminating with the highest emotional response last.

Feeling: _____

1. Possible thought generated by the brain:

" _____

_____ "

a. Emotional meaning assigned

_____

_____

2. Possible thought generated by the brain:

" _____

_____ "

(Better-feeling thought)

a. Emotional meaning assigned

" _____

_____ "

(Better-feeling emotion)

3. Possible thought generated by the brain:

" _____

_____ "

(Better-feeling thought)

a. Emotional meaning assigned

" _____

_____ "

(Better-feeling emotion)

Feeling: _____

1. Possible thought generated by the brain:

"_____

_____"

a. Emotional meaning assigned

_____

_____

2. Possible thought generated by the brain:

"_____

_____"

(Better-feeling thought)
a. Emotional meaning assigned

"_____

_____"

(Better-feeling emotion)

3. Possible thought generated by the brain:

"_____

_____"

(Better-feeling thought)
a. Emotional meaning assigned

"_____

_____"

(Better-feeling emotion)

Before we leave this conversation about the role of feelings, thoughts, and emotions, I want to be clear; ALL emotions are important for us to be aware of – they are our friends. We are not "bad people" if we are experiencing temporary despair, fear, overwhelm, or worry. In fact, it is extremely important for us to recognize our current emotional response. Only in this way are we able to receive the internal message and deliberately allow it to process through us. If we attempt to stuff the emotion or ignore it, it will ALWAYS find a way to resurface for us to manage, transform and release. Often times when it resurfaces, the stage on which it shows itself has a larger audience, so it is usually best to attempt to feel it fully when it comes around the first time. We are then free to choose a better-feeling emotion and better able to move forward.

MIRRORS

Mirrors are objects whereby we can observe a reflection of ourselves. They provide a faithful representation and/or image of the whole rather than a fragmented piece of our physical appearance. Reliable and valid, our reflection is sometimes pleasing and other times jarring. Let's extrapolate this concept of mirrors from the visual and physical representations of ourselves to something more internal; the people in our lives.

> "THE WHOLE PURPOSE OF EDUCATION
> IS TO TURN MIRRORS INTO WINDOWS."
> ~ SYDNEY J. HARRIS

Everyone in our immediate circle, both personally and professionally, act as mirrors reflecting back to us who we are being in any given moment. Think back to the exercise in the previous section...those thoughts and emotions we formulate upon witnessing behaviors in others are a result of people (the mirror) showing us something about ourselves. When we are with people who are complimenting us, showering us with praise, or in general helping us to feel good about ourselves, the reflection is pleasing.

However, when we are with people who we find to be arrogant, stubborn, or any other displeasing feeling, it can be because they are reflecting something back to us about ourselves that has possibly been repressed, triggering a chain reaction of emotions. This is often followed by self-talk that might sound like, "I can't stand that person", "Who do they think they are?", and on and on. In fact, these people are often our best teachers in life because they have caused something in us to come to the surface for purging, transforming or balancing in order for us to heal and move forward. As we shine a light on these charged emotions within, they soon dissipate and the people and situations that trigger them stop showing up in our lives.

One fair warning – if we attempt to hide from these mirrors when they show up for us, a larger mirror will follow up perhaps in a different way, so that we face what likely needs to be examined.

This may help to explain why similar people present themselves in our lives like patterns until we learn the lessons. Not to worry though, as we progress, we attract other mirrors with different lessons that help us learn and adjust accordingly. This is a simple concept, but one that can be challenging to navigate.

When we go into the school faculty lounge, meet with our teams, administration, parents, and others, we begin to tune into our thoughts and emotions while we are there. What is being mirrored back or triggered in us?

When you notice a positive trigger, how does that feel? Please describe.

When you notice a negative trigger, how does that feel? Please describe.

You have now called up to the surface a feeling to process/ transform and you are feeling it in your body. Take a deep breath, a long inhalation and a long exhalation. Repeat this breathing as many times as it takes you to begin to release this feeling. Know that it may take a couple of attempts to release it completely.

Now describe how you feel.

Another mirroring tool to help us reflect on our behavior is simply through the power of observation. And by that I do not mean having someone observe us, but that we view or observe ourselves. Why is this important and how does it help? Because physics has shown us that assuming the role of the observer impacts the outcome.

Using the example of the out of control student from the previous section, I have the capability to observe myself interacting with said student. What do I want to see? Would I like to observe myself becoming frustrated or angry with him or would I prefer to envision myself calmly finding a way to resolve the issue – the latter version more likely producing the desired outcome. We have the ability to observe ourselves while we are in the act of doing. How do we know and do this?

In 1803, what is often referred to as "The Most Beautiful Experiment in Physics" was conducted by Thomas Young. You may have also heard of this as the Double Slit Experiment. The basic premise of this experiment was to determine how energy and matter behave. Are they primarily waves or are they particles? In the past, the prevailing viewpoint was that they could only be one or the other. However, in the Double Slit Experiment, Thomas Young discovered that matter exhibits characteristics of BOTH waves and particles.

Scientists began replicating this experiment and each time the results were the same. By sending a beam of light at a piece of paper with two slits, they could observe a pattern on the plate behind it. However, the pattern that emerged confused the scientists. Instead of revealing two lines that paralleled the slits, it was a random pattern that indicated interference, or that the particles behaved like a wave.

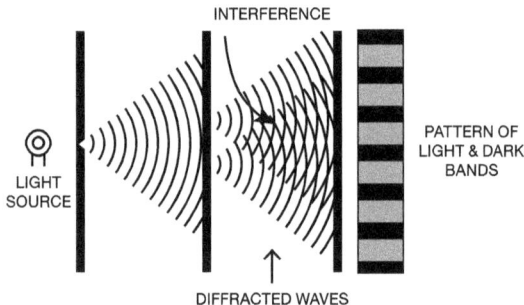

INTERFERENCE

LIGHT SOURCE

PATTERN OF LIGHT & DARK BANDS

DIFFRACTED WAVES

Conversely, when individual photons were sent through the slits one at a time, they arrived on the plate as a particle or in the formation of the slits – indicating the photons behaved as particles.

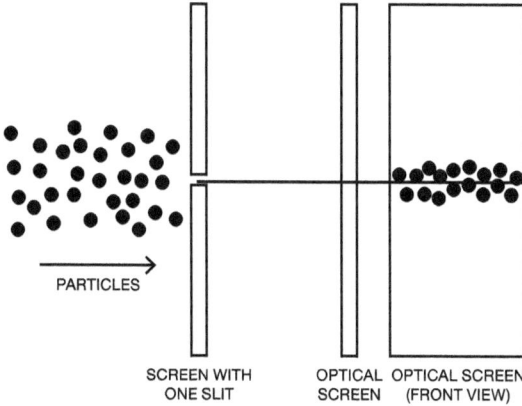

SCREEN WITH ONE SLIT   OPTICAL SCREEN   OPTICAL SCREEN (FRONT VIEW)

PARTICLES

Because these results were so confounding, they decided to observe and measure what happens at the exact moment when the photons pass through the double slit. Much to their surprise, their discovery indicated that *when observed,* light displays properties like that of a particle. *When not observed,* light appears as a wave. The light does not have an exact location in time and space until it is observed. So, what did we learn from this? The observer is the one who ultimately determines what form shows up. If the scientist is looking for a particle that is what is found. If the scientist is searching for a wave that is what is seen. Light has dualist properties depending solely on the observer effect. So what? What are the implications here for us?

The significance of the observer being the determining factor in the outcome of the experiment cannot be underscored enough. What this means is, by focusing our ability to observe a desired outcome in our mind, we can influence the outcome. When our thoughts and observations work together in harmony, we create or manifest the results we desire. How does that feel? Empowering? It should. Simply be present to the possibilities and become more aware in the moment.

Think of a student or an upcoming event where you would really like to ensure a positive outcome. Please describe.

Now, sitting quietly by yourself (please set aside about 2-5 minutes), close your eyes. While you are envisioning this student or event, watch yourself carry out your role in this interaction... leading to a highly successful conclusion. You are witnessing yourself and partnering your observation with a feeling of positive expectation or hopefulness, or maybe even joy. Please describe your actions and how you feel.

This is how you can choose to feel when the event actually takes place. At the conclusion of the event, please return to what you wrote above and compare what actually happened with your envisioning of it. Please describe.

INTENTIONAL WORD CHOICE

The words we speak not only carry meaning, they carry a vibration and an energy. In fact, our speech contains the power to create our reality. For many of us, we are creating our reality unconsciously. If we are unhappy or dissatisfied with our lives either personally or professionally, I suggest improving our skill set. Start creating at a more conscious level. If we are content with our personal and professional lives, then we can continue to refine our skills in this area in order to enhance our life experience. Even children know how to do this, they are just not likely to be conscious of it.

"ABRACADABRA – I CREATE AS I SPEAK."
~ AUTHOR UNKNOWN

I was away at a conference for a couple of days when my daughter, then a third grader, was about to participate in her second classroom spelling bee. As was customary when I was out of town, I would call home before she went to bed to check in and see how her day had gone. On the eve of the competition, I advised her to simply do her best and enjoy herself. Without even taking a breath, she declared that she was going to emerge as the winner the next day. Keep in mind she had already participated in a spelling bee a couple weeks before and did not win. As a mother, I did not want her to feel stressed out about this, in the event she didn't win. I did not want her to feel like she had in some way failed. I again simply encouraged her to do her best while she continued to insist she was going to be the first place finisher. What amazed me was that there was no anxiousness in her voice, just a very confident matter-of-fact statement.

The next day I could not wait until evening to call home. I called after school because I wanted to be there to help either pick up the pieces or congratulate her. Before I could even ask, she joyfully informed me that she took first place in the spelling bee. Make no mistake, this was not a "win" for ego purposes, this was a clear declaration of desire, where thought and feeling were combined and would not be denied. Nor can it ever be denied when there is definitiveness of purpose wrapped up in intentional word choice, and bathed in what it feels like when it happens. We create as we speak.

Now, the converse is also true. Have you ever thought any of the following comments?

1. I hope I don't screw this up.
2. This student needs a positive attitude.
3. I'm disappointed in you/myself.
4. Student has no desire to learn.
5. Lack of effort.
6. I'm so stressed.
7. This job is killing me.

Just reading that list and saying it out loud can generate a feeling of despair or possibly hopelessness. How can I convey the message AND do that in a way that uplifts so I am not drained of my energy? Try these:

1. I am capable of positively impacting the outcome here.
2. Student continues to work on improving their attitude.
3. I am learning from previous decisions and making better choices.
4. Student continues to work on applying him/herself to the learning objectives.
5. Working on increasing motivation.
6. I am going with the flow and know everything will be ok.
7. I am growing with each challenge I face in this job.

You may be laughing right now at how awkward it feels to make some of these statements. That in and of itself demonstrates we are not in the habit of phrasing things in ways that can help create a positive response to events, rather than exacerbate the negative. So, given that our intentional word choice creates what we experience, let's practice.

Please make a list of statements you have said recently or are habitual that leave you feeling drained, hopeless, or disempowered:

Now, take a few moments and rephrase these in a more positive way, or in a way that leaves you feeling lighter. You may wish to only complete one at a time and return to this exercise later.

After rewriting each of these, what have you noticed about your intentional word choice and how it makes you feel? Please describe.

RESISTANCE

Let's set the stage here by further exploring the meaning and substance of the concept of resistance. The first example of a synonym for the word *resistance* is *opposition*. Others listed are *obstinacy, defiance,* and *intransigence*. To further our depth of understanding, when reviewing antonyms of *resistance* we find *acceptance, capitulation, and compliance*. So, when I am in resistance to something, I am akin to a salmon swimming upstream, fighting the current. Not only is battling the forces of the water difficult, in some cases I perish while I am enroute to my birthplace. Stick with me here…I realize we are not fish and that is my point exactly. The cycle of the salmon run is instinctual, but we humans always have the capability to choose. So would we then choose to accept something that we find unacceptable or is causing us stress? Do we acquiesce, or even worse, surrender? No, there is a middle and significantly more powerful solution – BE present.

> "WHATEVER YOU FIGHT, YOU STRENGTHEN,
> AND WHAT YOU RESIST, PERSISTS."
> ~ E. TOLLE

When we spend our precious time and energy "arguing" with current reality as it is, we are adding fuel to an already burning flame. For example, let's take the issue of testing as that was identified as a big contributor to stress. As a teacher I can "choose" (we don't really realize we are choosing this, it is more an unconscious reaction) to complain and find fault with all aspects of testing both to myself and anyone who will listen all day every day, but to what end? I am in opposition to the present moment in which I find myself. This is always due to some form of regret or fear – regret from a past experience, or fear about some event in the future.

Conversely, it doesn't mean that we simply accept and surrender. When we are "being" present instead of arguing with what is, we can find ourselves at peace. Isn't coming from a peaceful place more likely to yield our desired results? Of course it is. If we are truly desirous of changing our circumstances as they are, then we should choose to come from this grounded, peaceful (present) place and with clarity, decide to take action. When we are present, in a state of non-judgement, we truly feel better and thus make better choices. How do we do this?

If you have ever had the experience of driving in ice and snow, there may have been a time when you temporarily lost control of the car. In a split second you can feel the vehicle sliding and you react very quickly. We usually react by steering the car in the opposite direction that we are sliding. If you have done this, you also realize that reaction exacerbates the problem. The car then loses control faster and you likely go into a 180 or 360 degree spin. The trick is to steer into the slide, or steer into the direction the car is moving. This of course seems counterintuitive while you are experiencing the loss of control, but once it happens to you a second, third, or however many times, you learn not to react, but to choose to direct the car into the spin. By doing this, you are able to regain control over the vehicle and in most cases go on your merry way. Resistance is the same. Instead of fighting it, or arguing with the situation as it currently is, steer into it. Be curious about it. Why am I feeling a battle brewing? Sit with the feeling for a while and consciously examine your thoughts and feelings about it. Only in this manner are we able to bring to the surface the cause or trigger of the resistance in order that we release it and return to a state of peace.

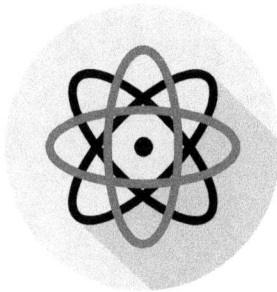

Consult your list of stressors from section one and choose one where you know you felt a state of resistance. Please describe.

Steer into that feeling of defiance or obstinacy. Is there something surfacing from the past, or is it more a worry about a future event? Please describe.

Acknowledge the thought and the feeling that accompanies the thought and sit with it for a few minutes. Now release them. Please describe how you are feeling about the identified stressor and report any changes.

Some of the issues we have experienced resistance towards may have been with us buried deeply for quite a long while so we may wish to repeat these steps again with the same topic. Or if we feel it has dissipated then select a different stressor and repeat the process.

TEACHERS REIGNITE THEIR PASSION TO INSPIRE!

"We become what we repeatedly do."
~ Sean Covey

We have now identified several ways to relieve and alleviate stress that is triggered by various events in our teaching careers. Obviously, these suggestions also serve to do the same when the triggers are generated in our personal lives as well. In order for these tools to be effective, we will need to commit to practicing them with enough frequency that they become new habits. Perhaps a more important reason we want to develop these routines on a daily basis is because with regular practice, we are then able to inoculate ourselves from the triggers. Put another way, we begin to develop an immunity to simply reacting to the stressors. Not only are we able to better manage our stress, we actually begin to *attract less of it.*

In order to keep this workable and increase our ability to be successful, we are going to develop these new habits via a two-pronged protocol:
Know What You Desire and 11:11:11 for 11 Repeat.

KNOW WHAT YOU DESIRE

This should be easy, right? What we want or desire is to feel and have less stress in our lives. But *are we willing* to do what is necessary to make that happen? Do we earnestly desire to alleviate the causes? Thomas Hobbes, a noted philosopher, suggested that desire is the fundamental motivation of all human action. If this is true, then we must feel a yearning to move emotional energy from the problem to the solution in order to transform the now. Let's repeat that. If we are dissatisfied enough with our current circumstances, we must feel a desire to move emotional energy from the problem to the solution in order to transform the now. When we get *very clear* on how we want to feel, the journey itself becomes infinitely more gratifying and the probability of experiencing the desired feelings increases exponentially.

We as humans are big bundles of energy. We also know from our science teachers that energy cannot be created or destroyed… it can only be directed. So in any given moment we are emitting energy. We are in a sense a *power source* of energy. And while we are this generator of energy, we are also *magnets*. What we attract to ourselves in fact matches what we radiate. It doesn't matter if we are aware of this fact or not, it's what is occurring. Now that we KNOW this, let's direct our energy *consciously* with clarity, so we can *create* the experiences we desire.

The first step in directing our energy is to identify how we wish to feel. How do we want to feel when we are in our classrooms, teaching, working with colleagues, conferencing with parents/administrators, etc.? In order to best tap into our feelings, we are going to begin with a gratitude exercise. Why is that? Because it is hard to feel or express negativity when we are grateful. Before creating this list, find something symbolic to keep with you. This could be a shell, small stone, or seed; something large enough to hold yet small enough to carry with you. I'll explain this part later.

If you've never created a gratitude list before, here are some suggestions: a list can be generated in categories, for example: relationships, money, love, health, work, general success, creativity, etc. These ideas are merely here to assist in getting the juices flowing. Use them if it is helpful, or create your own.

Gratitude statements can be formatted in several different ways.

Here are some examples I have previously used:

I am so grateful for _____
because _____

I am truly thankful for _____
because _____

I am so blessed to have _____
because _____

I am so happy and excited for _____
because _____

I am so grateful for _____
because _____

I am truly thankful for _____
because _____

I am so blessed to have _____
because _____

I am so happy and excited for _____
because _____

You can choose one of these, all of them, or any combination of whatever feels best to you. The reason it is important to add the "because" tag at the end of the statement is to deepen the feeling. The sensation of gratitude is enhanced when we include the *why* with it. In doing so, we begin to transform the now.

Next, create a list of 55 statements. It is helpful to be in a quiet place with plenty of time to complete this from start to finish.

1. _____

2. _____

3. _____

4. _____

5. _____

6. _____

7. _____

8. _____

9. _____

10. _____

11. _____

12. _____

13. _____

14. _____

15. _____

16. _____

17. _____

18. _____

19. _____

20. _____

21. _____

22. _____

23. _____

24. _____

25. _____

26. _____

27. _____

28. _____

29. _____

30. _____

31. _____

32. _____

33. _____

34. _____

35. _____

36. _____

37. _____

38. _____

39. _____

40. _____

41. _____

42. _____

43. _____

44. _____

45. _____

46. _____

47. _____

48. _____

49. _____

50. _____

51. _____

52. _____

53. _____

54. _____

55. _____

Once your personal gratitude list is completed, take your symbol into your hand and read each of your 55 statements out loud followed by the words *thank you.*

Keeping your symbol near you, write a couple of statements, or a summary articulating how you feel now after creating your gratitude list.

Summary:

From this elevated sense of well-being emerges our intention to feel better and help bring that improved emotional state to the present moment. Now, every night before going to sleep, place your symbol on your nightstand and look at it. Celebrate the ability to create and shift the way we feel in any given moment. In the morning when you awake, again, look at and feel your symbol. Begin your day with the feelings of gratitude that you created and are creating.

You may also choose to carry your symbol with you during the day, in your pocket or to have available somewhere close by in order to serve as a reminder of your gratefulness.

At a certain point, you will no longer need this symbol, as it will have served its purpose – a visual and physical reminder that we choose how we feel in any given moment. And whatever that feeling is, we have the ability to fully feel it in the moment and then select something that feels better.

11:11:11
FOR 11 REPEAT

It has been suggested that when we are depressed we are living in the past. When we are anxious we are living in the future. *Only in the present do we find our personal power and have the ability to effect change.* When we choose to take focused action with intention in our daily rituals, there are no limits to what we can do. No limits.

As we begin new habits, it is important to create a process to follow with a visual reminder so the first steps to change are easier to manage and we can witness our success. It may also be helpful to implement this protocol with a partner. You can support one another and thereby deepen your commitment through daily practice. The process I am outlining here is a format I created for myself over a period of years. This is a version of what I follow and have habituated on a **daily** basis:

11 Minutes of Quiet Time/Meditation/Breathing
11 Minutes of Positive Reading/Listening
11 Minutes of Physical Activity/Breathing
11 Days in a Row

Repeat this pattern five additional times for a total of 66 days.

If you are like most people, you may look at this schedule and think, *"I absolutely do not have 33 minutes I can add to my day."* Life has become exceptionally busy and moves faster all the time, so let's frame this in a different way. *"How can I plan my day around these 33 minutes?"*

If I know I can reduce my stress, feel better and manage myself more effectively by practicing these daily habits, I commit myself to this 11 day process five times and look for the results. Let's remember one very important thing – you schedule these three 11 minute activities according to what works best for you. I will share where I fit them into my day, but that may or may not be the same for you.

11 MINUTES OF QUIET TIME/ MEDITATION/BREATHING

This is how I begin my day. After giving thanks for another day, I find a quiet place to sit and focus on my breath and my connection with life. Admittedly, when I began this was terribly challenging. When we run 100 miles an hour every day, sitting quietly actually seems unnerving…at first. It may take several days or weeks in a row for you to begin to feel your mind quiet down. This is completely normal.

There is no way to fail at this unless you give up and quit. Stay committed to these 11 minutes daily and here is what begins to happen – positive physiological changes take place in the body. For example, daily meditation is linked to a decrease in cortisol (our stress hormone), improved sleep, reduction in blood pressure, and vast shifts in brain function.

Our frontal cortex tends to go "offline" and gives our brain a rest. The thalamus, our gatekeeper for the senses, reduces the flow of incoming information to a trickle, allowing for space between thought and action. The brain's reticular formation, or arousal area, is dialed back when we meditate regularly. Imagine having the ability to choose NOT to engage in fight or flight behavior, or reduce the frequency of engagement when these moments present themselves (students, parents, administrators, etc.).

There are actually many other benefits to a daily quiet time/ meditation too numerous to elaborate on. Just do your own homework and give it a try. You will be able to generate your own list of how this positively benefits you and more importantly, helps you feel better.

11 MINUTES OF POSITIVE READING/LISTENING

The basic premise of this section is...garbage in, garbage out. What am I feeding myself? Do I allow negativity rent-free space in my head? If the answer is yes, I need to reflect on why and address how to change it.

What I do know is I can become more positive by increasing my daily diet of things that inspire me. I usually dedicate these 11 minutes to the very end of my day, or right before going to sleep. In fact, the last five minutes of our day may well be the most important five minutes of all. Our subconscious processes our last waking thoughts before drifting off to sleep, like a good tea steeping. Being aware of this, I am careful to feed my subconscious something that feels good.

Now, if you are like me, some nights I am just too tired to read anything and fall asleep as soon as my head hits the pillow. If that describes you, you may choose to listen to 11 minutes of something uplifting instead. This can happen anywhere – driving in the car, during a walk, etc. There are so many options it is difficult to mention them all. Let's just share a few: recorded books, music, meditations, positive affirmations, TED Talks, and speeches by inspiring people.

It is also important to note that I might decide to read for five minutes and listen to material for six minutes. That is perfectly fine. You may break up these 11 minutes in any way that serves you, just aim for a total of 11 minutes daily to fill yourself up with positive and inspiring content. In some cases, these 11 minutes can potentially also be happening concurrently with the next 11 minute activity.

11 MINUTES OF PHYSICAL ACTIVITY/BREATHING

We have long known the benefits of physical activity on the body, however the relationship between mind and body is becoming increasingly better understood. Regular exercise has a profoundly positive impact on reducing anxiety, depression, and helping the body process and dissolve emotions. When exercise is interwoven into our daily routine, we strengthen our body **and** our cognitive functioning. *It is important to note that if you have any type of health issue, to please check with your medical practitioner before beginning a new routine.* So what is meant by physical activity?

Again, there are so many options here, these 11 minutes are very easy to plan our day around. This can be as easy as simple stretching exercises, walking, running, yoga, weights, etc. There are many stretching exercises that involve very simple moves. Keep it simple and begin with easy things. All activity that is practiced regularly has a direct impact on improved mental health, sharper memory and thinking, better sleep, a reduction in stress and anxiety, and an increase in energy. This is not about suffering, but about maintaining our bodies and minds at maximum capacity. Do your homework here and you will have your own success stories to share.

A visual reminder of this process can look like this.

Days	11 min Quiet Time	11 min Reading/Listening	11 min Physical Activity
Day 1			
Day 2			
Day 3			
Day 4			
Day 5			
Day 6			
Day 7			
Day 8			
Day 9			
Day 10			
Day 11			

Days	11 min Quiet Time	11 min Reading/Listening	11 min Physical Activity
Day 1			
Day 2			
Day 3			
Day 4			
Day 5			
Day 6			
Day 7			
Day 8			
Day 9			
Day 10			
Day 11			

Days	11 min Quiet Time	11 min Reading/Listening	11 min Physical Activity
Day 1			
Day 2			
Day 3			
Day 4			
Day 5			
Day 6			
Day 7			
Day 8			
Day 9			
Day 10			
Day 11			

Days	11 min Quiet Time	11 min Reading/Listening	11 min Physical Activity
Day 1			
Day 2			
Day 3			
Day 4			
Day 5			
Day 6			
Day 7			
Day 8			
Day 9			
Day 10			
Day 11			

Days	11 min Quiet Time	11 min Reading/Listening	11 min Physical Activity
Day 1			
Day 2			
Day 3			
Day 4			
Day 5			
Day 6			
Day 7			
Day 8			
Day 9			
Day 10			
Day 11			

Days	11 min Quiet Time	11 min Reading/Listening	11 min Physical Activity
Day 1			
Day 2			
Day 3			
Day 4			
Day 5			
Day 6			
Day 7			
Day 8			
Day 9			
Day 10			
Day 11			

This chart can be copied and posted anywhere that is convenient for you to reaffirm your daily commitment to yourself and these practices. Place a checkmark in the columns at the end of each day. If for some reason a day or a category is missed, simply begin again and *refrain from self-judgment*. The intention is to begin a daily practice, not beat yourself up for "failing" to complete the habits. You will soon find you are looking forward to these daily appointments and taking good care of yourself. This is the beginning of extreme self-care. We can only give to others what we ourselves possess. I wish to share with my students, parents, colleagues, and administrators the best of me, so I begin my honoring myself first.

FOLLOW-UP

The most effective way to ensure our success in managing our stress and improving our overall well-being is to build in follow-up or check-ins. The visual reminder chart previously shown is to be used for individual daily monitoring of creating new habits. However, the main idea is to see our new habits shifting the way we feel, and additionally, improving how we experience our daily lives in schools.

In closing, when asking teachers to suggest something they feel would make things better moving forward, there was a response that contained an amalgamation of most thoughts:

"WE NEED TO EXPERIENCE A WAY OF BEING LEARNERS. WE LEARN FROM OUR OWN TEACHERS AND INSTEAD OF ATTENDING MORE LECTURES, TEACHERS SHOULD PARTICIPATE IN HANDS-ON APPLICATIONS AND FACILITATE FOR THEIR OWN LEARNING POSSIBILITIES."

This is my highest wish for all of us.

Debbie Ford says it beautifully, *"I think that any time of great pain is a time of transformation, a fertile time to plant new seeds."*

So let us begin sowing by committing to begin each day with renewed gratitude. See yourself into a new way of being by knowing how you want to feel and practicing 11:11:11 for 11 Repeat five times. You will not lose all the stress in your life, but your ability to manage it will improve dramatically, and that my friend will make your days in school more joyful.

Have faith and believe in your ability to Reignite Your Passion to Inspire!

7 KEYS TO REDUCE STRESS AND REFUEL YOUR TANK

1st Key
BREATHE

Tune into and become conscious of your breathing in any given moment. Pay attention to the rate (fast, slow) and depth (shallow, deep). Oftentimes when we feel stress, changes in our breathing are the first physical manifestations that occur in tandem with an accelerated heart rate.

When you are in a situation where you are noticing these physical sensations, step back and consciously BREATHE – focus on inhaling more slowly with longer exhalations. This is a great starting point to simply relaxing a bit, reducing the tension your body is feeling, and moving forward in a more powerful, controlled manner.

Give it a try and see how it feels!

What situations or challenges cause you to hold your breath or have shallow breathing? How does it feel when you take deep breaths and feel the tension leave your body?

2nd Key
CREATE SPACE

"BETWEEN STIMULUS AND RESPONSE
THERE IS A SPACE.
IN THAT SPACE IS OUR POWER
TO CHOOSE OUR RESPONSE.
IN OUR RESPONSE LIES OUR GROWTH
AND OUR FREEDOM."
~ VICTOR FRANKL

When we are in the middle of a stressful situation, oftentimes we are in react mode. A different approach is to RESPOND. What makes it possible to respond instead of react is to create a margin of space in between the trigger of stress and our response to it.

Try it out. When you feel the stress coming on, check in with yourself and step back – BREATHE - then CHOOSE your response. We can make this happen by creating just a little bit of space!

What situations or challenges cause you to react? How does it feel when you take a deep breath and consciously choose your response? Do you experience a difference outcome?

3rd Key
RECONNECT

When we reconnect to a larger sense of purpose, many stressful events begin to melt away. Take the position of observing yourself the next time you are in the middle of a situation that triggers stress.

Do you like what you see? Am I reacting or responding? Is my larger sense of purpose here to spew negative words, or does this truly matter in the big picture?

Try reconnecting to your bigger sense of purpose if you feel tension begin to present itself!

When faced with stressful situations or challenges, how do you react or respond? Does focusing on your purpose change your reaction?

4th Key
INVENTORY – EMOTIONS

Notice your emotional state. Our emotions range from despair to joy with everything in between. Ask yourself, am I in a state of despair? Anger? Frustration? Know that wherever you are at any given moment is ok. Just in the awareness of it, consciously CHOOSE to feel just a bit better.

In so choosing we move from a sense of disempowerment to empowerment.

Next time you feel stressed, take a very quick inventory of how you feel, notice that feeling, and choose to feel better!

What situations or challenges cause you to feel disempowered?
What choices can you make to feel empowered?

5th Key
INVENTORY – WORDS

"THE QUALITY OF YOUR COMMUNICATION
SHAPES THE QUALITY OF YOUR LIFE.
EVERY CELL IN YOUR BEING ALIGNS WITH
WHAT YOU DECLARE."
~ NIURKA

Notice your words! Be very aware that we create as we speak. Am I making my stressful situation worse by my words or story I am telling? If I am committed to reducing stress and refueling my tank, I am consciously aware of the words I speak.

When you feel yourself succumbing to tension, breathe, and tell yourself (preferably out loud) that you let go of any stress and tension, and immediately notice you feel better!

What situations or challenges cause you to think or say disempowering words? When you release the tension, what does your inner or outer dialogue sound like?

6th Key
SILENCE

One way to dramatically reduce those things/events in our lives that trigger stress is to dedicate a small amount of time daily to just be silent. If this is new to you start small, maybe 2-3 minutes. Once that is in place, build up to more time, ideally 15-20 minutes per day.

Reconnecting to our inner wisdom on a regular basis has a calming effect that directly impacts our emotional response to outer events. Eventually the triggers dissipate and often disappear altogether.

Try it out beginning today, for 2-3 minutes. It's a gift to yourself because YOU are worth it!

What does it feel like to experience silence? Are you able to do it with ease, or is it difficult to quiet your inner dialogue? Once you dissipate the stress triggers, are you able to reduce your overall stress level?

7th Key
MOVE

Stress and tension are all forms of energy. When we feel these things in and around us, a great way to alleviate it is to physically move. Try taking a walk, a run, or simply stretch your body. Any type of physical movement will actually force it to pass through us more quickly.

Physical activity when practiced on a regular basis can also assist with preventing stress to manifest in the first place.

Get your body moving and see how you respond next time stress begins to present itself!

What situations or challenges cause you to feel stress or tension?
How does physical activity affect your stress level?

ABOUT

ELIZABETH ROSADO-MCGRATH, MEd

Elizabeth Rosado-McGrath, MEd hails from the Twin Cities (near Lake Wobegon) and attended the University of Minnesota. After graduation she headed to San Antonio, Texas in her quest to become a bilingual and ESL teacher. Eventually settling in Houston, Liz worked in public schools for 20 plus years having the privilege of serving in many roles from classroom teacher to several administrative positions. She completed her master's in education at Houston Baptist University and continued her doctoral studies in curriculum and instruction at the University of Houston. Liz is listed in *Who's Who in American Education* and was previously nominated for Bilingual Teacher of the Year.

Having spent time as a student in low reading groups in elementary school, Liz developed a passion for struggling readers and working with teachers of challenging students. Thus, her love of coaching educators and professional development was born. She became a *Seven Habits of Highly Effective People* trainer and a student of Cognitive Coaching. This ultimately led to her work as an educational consultant and the creation of Transformed Teachers where she is currently President. Liz is also a charter member of Lessons from Experts and her page Lessons from Educators is housed there.

From Burned Out to Fired Up is Liz's first solo authored book. Previously published works include a co-authored chapter in *Multicultural and Multilingual Literacy and Language*, and co-authored selections in *Zoe Life Inspired 2016*.

Liz currently resides in Houston with her family and sweet dog, a chug named Walby while traveling extensively as an Educational Consultant.

TRANSFORMED TEACHERS

TEACHERS REIGNITE THEIR PASSION TO INSPIRE

ELIZABETH ROSADO-MCGRATH, MEd

Workshops and Coaching available for teachers.
Struggling with stress?
Learn tools to manage and reduce stress,
refuel your tank, and experience more joy in teaching!

Reignite your passion to inspire with:
Group Coaching
1:1 Coaching
Refuel Your Joy

To book Liz Rosado-McGrath for workshops or coaching,
Contact her at:
281-507-0049 or LizMSP@Yahoo.com

LET'S CONNECT!

Facebook.com/TransformedTeachers
@TransformedTeachers
#TransformedTeachers
www.TransformedTeachers.net